SUGAR SANDWICH

My Affair With Food:
Delectable & Dialect-able Tales!

by Diane Wells Rivers

AuthorHouse™
1663 Liberty Drive
Bloomington, IN 47403
www.authorhouse.com
Phone: 1-800-839-8640

Published by AuthorHouse 7/25/2012

ISBN: 978-1-4685-2464-2 (sc)

Book cover design by Nicholas Daniel Dean Rivers
Nick Rivers is a graphic artist and designer who was born in Omaha, Nebraska, and now resides in New Smyrna Beach, Florida.
rivtothecore@gmail.com

Library of Congress Control Number: 2011962643

Any people depicted in stock imagery provided by Thinkstock are models,
and such images are being used for illustrative purposes only.
Certain stock imagery © Thinkstock.

This book is printed on acid-free paper.

authorHOUSE®

Contents

Diane Wells Rivers

Taste the sweetness between the bread. Jam to the tales of deliciousness!

Sugar Sandwich © is dedicated to the loving memory of my parents, Elizabeth and Clarence Wells, and my ten brothers and sisters.

We grew up poor, but the richness of the experience led us to succeed in a variety of careers, from business owner to master seamstress, truck driver, banker, nurse, and educator.

This book is also dedicated to Ron, my husband and our children, Gabriel, Marcus, and Nicholas.

Introduction

HEREIN LIE THE juicy details of my affair with food, held long before cooking became a nationally televised pastime. I chose the word *affair* because it embodies my family's relationship with food: illicit, indulgent, scandalous, and oftentimes hidden from the view of others. Our family loves food, and we usually use food as love.

Americans' passion for food continues today, and its legacy will be passed on to our children. This is a testimony of how memories of food sustain our spirit and sense of family and how eating certain foods can elicit many moods.

From the preparation of the fatted calf to the breaking of bread, we take daily sustenance. Food nourishes our physical bodies and strengthens our cultural fiber. Our choice of foods can be shaped by region, climate, availability, and preference. The foods we serve can, in turn, shape the events in our lives and leave a permanent imprint on our souls.

So name and claim your "sugar sandwich." What's yours? Is it a fried apple pie with homemade ice cream? A warm brownie with pecans? Whatever your "sugar sandwich," enjoy one today!

—Diane

Christmas 2009: Diane had been cooking—covered dishes, cookies, candy, pies—but a big snow storm meant no one was able to come over and enjoy them … except for Diane and her husband, Ron. (Personal photo ©)

Chapter 1

PASSION, FOOD, AND MARRIAGE

FOOD IS INTENSELY and passionately personal. Our food choices are linked to our most intimate memories, and our eating habits reveal what makes us happy, sad, lonely, or excited. When my husband, Ron, buys a can of cashews, he smiles and licks his lips with anticipation. I also have seen him grimace when I attempt to make oatmeal or sweet tea a part of his diet. Once when I was on a trip out of town to Minneapolis, Ron told me he purchased my favorite foods because he missed me. And if we see a platter of shrimp, we both get excited!

When a person shops for food—touches it, smells it, pays for it—a relationship is forged. An even stronger bond is formed when she grows it! During our many summers growing food in our backyard gardens, Ron and I have enjoyed the softness of the okra pods, the smell of fresh-picked, vine-ripened tomatoes, and the joy of harvesting baskets filled with jalapeños. Our joy begins the minute we walk into the nursery and choose our seedlings for the future harvest.

Japanese eggplants and striped zucchini become our friends and allies as we feed them with Miracle-Gro and water each day. Like our children, they grow and make us proud.

One of my adult memories of food that has influenced my emotions took place back in 1974, when Ron and I were newlyweds living on an army base. We ate a lot of green beans back then, and even now the smell of canned green beans brings back memories of our early marriage: poverty and army housing. To this day, I do not like to touch, smell, buy, cook, or taste canned green beans! Each time they are served, I relive the memories of sleeping on an army cot, living in small-town Missouri, and missing my family and friends. It doesn't matter how great the potato salad, fried chicken, or other parts of the meal are; canned green beans mean monotony, loneliness, isolation, and not enough money. For me, smells can conjure up memories better than photos can.

On the other hand, food also is associated with abundance, and certain foods conjure up some of my fondest childhood memories from early childhood. From 1964 to1968, we enjoyed a period of richness between our leaner times. When I smell fried homemade pork sausages or pork chops, baked ham, or anything from a pig, I think about money, happy times, people laughing, family reunions, and Momma and Daddy!

When I was growing up, our family's annual trip to the home farm in Vidalia, Georgia, meant good news: Momma and Daddy were agreeing on something, they would see their families, and they had enough money to drive us from Florida to Georgia. It also meant that we would have lots of good, fresh peas, corn, tomatoes, pears, beef, and butchered pork. The downside to all this was more work for my skinny little fingers. I would spend hours shelling field peas, peeling gigantic pears, and slicing tomatoes with my momma.

Our family's poverty was often situational, as was that of most black folk down South. When my daddy was able to make overtime as a brick mason or my momma had saved up some money from doing day work or cleaning white folks' houses, then we could afford the "extras," like gas for the car. Then there was money to go up to Vidalia to see our kin and get some fresh-from-the-farm food. When I was growing up in 1960s, my snacks consisted of fried sweet potatoes, home fries, raw turnip roots, and peach and apple fritters; I used to covet the Snickers, Now and Laters, and Cheetos my classmates brought to school.

Diane and her "peoples," 1974: Ron and Diane. (Personal photo 2010 ©)

Now that I can afford to eat anything I wish and shop anywhere I choose, my past relationships with food continue to influence my present food choices. While travel and exposure to new cuisine have had a tremendous influence on what I now cook and eat, I still reject foods with negative cultural connections to my youth. Those include the tiny cans of vienna sausages, canned mackerel, and fried bologna sandwiches associated with going fishing. As a child I disliked going fishing because of the mosquitoes and june bugs and sitting in the car in the hot Florida sun. Another reason I disliked fishing was because I hated bridges. Momma sat under tall bridges in order to cast her fishing line so she could catch angel fish and sea bass, and I dreaded bringing her shrimp bait while she sat under a bridge. This experience only added to my large collection of phobias and my dietary don'ts.

My Midwest-bred husband gets a look of sheer contentment on his face when the platter in front of him is piled with home-fried potatoes and onions with a sunny-side-up egg on top. He is at peace, comforted by the memories of his grandmother Emma and his mom, Dean. Ron loves to reminisce about how his grandmother would make him this dish and call him "King." He also remembers his mother, Emma Dean, making him this dish when he was a child, and giving him a loving look as she fried the potatoes. This cholestrol-laden meal is Ron's ultimate comfort food .

We all have our giddy moments brought on by food memories. Mine occurs when I go back home to Georgia and eat a slice of the seven-layer caramel-pecan cake that my Aunt Ginny makes. Her meal of super-sized drumsticks, better-than-store-bought potato salad, collard greens with chunks of ham, and hand-squeezed lemonade were to die for. Now new culinary fusions from my recent travels have been hard-wired into my frontal lobes. Mango salsa with pork chops, pan-fried sea scallops with linguine—and did I say pork chops?—are just some of my present-past combinations.

Chapter 2

BUTTERFLY KISSES AND DESSERTS (XOXO, RUTH AND DIANE)

SWEET TEA, SWEETBREADS, and sweet corn bread are down-home delicacies—although one of them is not so sweet! (Take a guess ... or Google to find out which one.) As children, my siblings and I were skinny little nothings; eating a hunk of chocolate cake, two slices of pie, and four or five peach fritters after a meal didn't show on our string-bean bodies. Back then, dessert meant your momma loved you enough to go the extra mile and make you the ultimate comfort food—warm, rich, sugary, and gooey. Nothing came from the box—it was all from scratch. We would salivate when we smelled fried apple pies, banana fritters, cocoa cake, tea cakes, plain cakes, and bread pudding.

When the month outlasted the ingredients, we scrounged, using canned freestone cling peaches and sweet dough to make a cobbler for the day's dessert. Leaner days found us stirring up corn cakes with cane syrup for a topping. We didn't miss Ms. Sara Lee, Mr. Duncan Hines, Ms. Marie Callender, or Lady Swanson, because we didn't know them.

Savoring a slice of just-baked cake all buttery brown from the oven was like getting a butterfly kiss and a hug from your mom. You took it for granted at the time, but later you realized that she didn't have a mixer; she just beat the hell out of that homemade batter with her strong arms—two hundred, three hundred, five hundred beats! Her black cast-iron pan baked the cake to perfection; the first bite said, "I love you," and the last bite was a sad good-bye to a close friend.

SWEET SISTER (AS TOLD BY RUTH) ...

My sister Diane's cheesecake is a slice of heaven. Her one-inch homemade crust, fluffy filling, and luscious fruit toppings could put a restaurant out of business. Her cheesecake, along with our momma's buttery 7-Up cakes, are my past and present dessert memories. Recently, Diane made a butter-rum bread pudding with caramel sauce, and I traveled across town to take 90 percent of it home with me. Her sons and husband do not eat bread pudding—their loss, my gain. Even if they did, I got to this one first and last. So smack,smack and yum, yum!

By now you may have decided that I am a foodaholic and need an intervention. On the contrary, I am a healthy-looking, beautiful, active woman who makes a conscious effort to balance my food-mood swings with lots of antioxidants, fiber, and protein. Sweetness, for me, is both sensory and spiritual. It's a day or an afternoon creating memories and good stuff to eat. I am a baker, and I create cardamom, oatmeal, and chocolate chip cookies for holidays and gift-giving. I feel and convey warmth with my generous gifts of time and love, and I take comfort in the confines of my pumpkin-colored kitchen. With forty years of expertise and skill, I create sweetness for my family and friends.

Chapter 3

MEMORIES OF BEING EIGHT AND ATE

MY SIBLINGS AND I loved riding in the back of the family's green 1962 Chevy station wagon with a shoebox full of sausage sandwiches, headed to Vidalia, Georgia. We would lie on handmade quilts, looking up at the tall white pine trees that guarded the dark highways. We didn't have any rest stops or fast-food breaks; Daddy drove straight through miles of Georgia red clay and up to our Grandma Florence's swept-dirt front yard. That annual pilgrimage to Georgia brought us face to face with our source of protein: cows, hogs, and chickens.

Grandma's front porch was an elevated veranda with no railings, made of the same pine that lined the highways. My imagination had conjured up giant chickens and miniature cows that lived underneath the porch; they would pounce on me—and only me—if I didn't scurry quickly up the brick steps. Once we were inside, southern hospitality took hold with hugs and kisses and a "How y'all been?" The catching up on who all the chillin' were and who was the knee baby slowly subsided as the aroma of supper took hold. My grandma and Ginny, our youngest aunt, had prepared a king's feast for us. We sat at a long pine table with pine benches on either side; there had to be twelve or more of us sitting there. Heavy-laden with farm-fresh fried chicken, shelled peas, fresh corn, sliced tomatoes, homemade biscuits, and potato salad, the table groaned, squeaked, and sighed as food was passed. Of course, no southern meal is complete without dessert, and Ginny's sky-high caramel-pecan butter cake satisfied my eternal sweet tooth.

Once all the cleaning and putting away was done, we chillin' had to take baths on the back porch using heated well water and homemade soap. My fear was not that someone would see my shiny, skinny nakedness ... no, my fear was that those giant chickens and miniature cows would jump out from under the porch and make me their supper! But the pitch darkness of the farm night and the flickering of june bugs melted away as my big sister and Momma stood guard. Their presence brought me peace of mind and soothed my monster fears. Later that night, I would sleep without a care in my grandmother's fluffy iron bed. It was so tall I had to climb into it using a footstool! And Momma brought me an inside potty to put by the bed so I wouldn't have to venture to the outhouse. Who knew if those giant and miniature farm monsters lived under there, too?

Chapter 4

SOME PEOPLE HAD TO MAKE DO—WE DID, TOO

ROGER—*MY DEAR OLDER* brother by two years—was the king of creative cooking when we were growing up in Jacksonville, Florida. Roger is my big brother in every sense of the word: he made up mean names for me, he took care of me at school (meaning he didn't let anyone else call me names—that was his exclusive privilege), and he was the first person other than a teacher to praise me publicly for my good grades and academic skills. (He also frequently requested that I "share" my homework with him.)

When I was in first grade, Rog would make my school lunch. His repertoire consisted of peanut butter, bologna—the kind you cut yourself—and jelly (usually grape). My momma would include an apple, cut in half and wrapped in waxed paper. Once I got to school, the cut part of the apple was brown from oxidation, and I, with my minimal science knowledge, assumed it was rotten. Like the crybaby that I was and am, I cried and refused to eat it, secretly coveting the school lunches of my well-off peers and embarrassed by my own lunch combo: sandwich and rotten apple.

If you're wondering why I didn't prepare my own lunch or why Momma didn't dip the apple in salt water or lemon juice, I don't know either. But it was a traumatic experience for a five-year-old entering the unfamiliar world of school, hot lunches, and a million newfound reasons to cry.

Rog had to walk me to school during my elementary years. In middle school I rode the bus, but Rog chose to walk with his entourage of friends. His reasons, I later learned, included mayhem, mischief, scamming lunch money, and an overall need to appear cool without being confined to a school bus. He was way smarter than I was about those things.

In the summertime, Rog delighted in attending neighborhood "rent" parties, jumping the fence to play or fight with his friends, and competing with me and my sister as we made homemade cookies, fried peach pies, and shrimp fried rice made from leftover fish bait. One time, Rog created this giant ball of dough concocted from our momma's flour and (I think) Crisco—the same stuff he used on his Gil Scott-Heron afro. His dough involved no baking powder, no sugar, and no butter. Needless to say, Rog's culinary ambition was rubbed in our faces as we made our meager sugar cookies and he shaped his soccer-ball-sized masterpiece. However, once he baked his creation in our gas oven and we taste-tested the monstrosity, with its glue-like flavor and missing ingredients, it took all the hot air out of Rog's previous braggadocio. We spat out the flour-and-water mess and ate our warm sugar cookies with twice the delight.

In between our various kitchen creations, we all managed to make snack-worthy fried butter and sugar sandwiches. Sometimes we'd add a little cinnamon; other times, straight-up cane sugar on light bread was all we needed until dinnertime. Even the mishaps I remember with fondness, treasuring how scarcity forced us to become creative and form lifelong bonds!

I once traced my family roots on my daddy's side back to 1865. I have since learned that Bert and Susie Wells were the parents of my grandaddy Elisha Wells. The Wells are a large group with a strong sense of family. We have been holding family reunions for eighty-five years.

My momma's people, the Fullers, came from the Carolinas and were part of the people called "Geechee" or "Gullah." The Fullers own land in Georgia that has been in our family for over one hundred years.

I encourage everyone to share a cup of tea or a slice of cake with a wise relative or two and find out who they are, what makes them strong, and what dreams they dreamed. You might find yourself in their roots!

Chapter 5

ABUNDANCE

CAWN IN DA Fannuh: Gullah Speak for "Corn in the Basket" or "A Good Harvest"

If you head south of the Mason-Dixon Line, then southeast, and then a little to the left near the St. John's River, you will find my heart and soul—the place where I learned to can tomatoes, put up peas, and make pear preserves.

Sistahs still do home canning! Why not start a blog about it or place *that* on your Facebook or Myspace page—I challenge you!

Here's a "summer abundance" recipe for all those tomatoes and peppers your well-meaning friends and neighbors give you at the end of summer. Your kitchen countertop can hold them for only so long, so why not create a salsa worthy of the best corn chips?

This salsa is one of my favorites to make—and one of Ron's favorites to eat. We get together and chop and taste the entire afternoon; he does the peppers, and I do everything else. I love the smells, the beautiful pint jars, and the gift labels I place on the lids. And my friends love receiving a jar of my homemade salsa.

Picante Salsa à la Diane

1 sweet onion, chopped

1 large sweet bell pepper, seeded and chopped

2 large jalapeños, seeded and chopped

1 large red pepper, seeded and chopped

5 cups chopped fresh tomatoes

2 T ground black pepper

2 cloves garlic, chopped fine

¼ cup sea salt

½ cup sugar

¼ cup lemon juice

Place all ingredients into a stainless steel pot. Bring to a boil, reduce heat, and simmer for 20 minutes. Cool and store in plastic containers or canning jars (using hot water bath per canning instructions). Makes 8–9 cups.

Ron and I enjoy cooking together so much. He doesn't mind doing the dishes if I cook his favorite dishes, and sometimes I'll create a favorite dish on the spot. My Chicken Curry Squash Stir Fry came from one of those times. The flavors are so good with a plate of jasmine rice, and if you've been blessed with too many yellow and zucchini squash, it makes for another great "summer abundance" recipe:

CHICKEN CURRY SUMMER SQUASH STIR FRY

2 yellow crookneck squash, sliced and then coarsely chopped

1 medium zucchini, chopped

1 large onion, chopped

3 green onions, chopped

1–2 lbs. chicken breast, cooked and chopped

½ cup curry powder

black pepper

garlic powder

paprika

1 red pepper, chopped and seeded

¼ cup olive oil

Cook chicken in a pan with olive oil, remove from pan, and set aside. Place onions in the pan, sauté, and then add the other vegetables and finally the seasonings. Stir-fry until tender but not overcooked. Add chicken back in and serve over jasmine rice.

A friend of mine, Kay, simply fell in love with my salsa and gave me the following accolades, which I am very happy to share:

Oh my gosh!!! That salsa was absolutely delicious. We have been gone a couple of days or I would have written you sooner. Chuck and I dived into it that evening, had our daughter, Natasha, and husband over to sample. Our son stopped by and sampled it. His family came to dinner on Sunday along with another couple, and Andy took that precious salsa out (I was conserving it for Chuck and me) and served it, and they raved about it. Do you share recipes? I would love to have it and make a barrel of it. Can it be frozen? It has an unusual taste, a little sweetness which is wonderful. I cannot wait to eat it again.

So, with Ron having planted fifteen tomato plants and twenty-one pepper plants, I decided to unload—uh, I mean, share.

WHAT DO PEPPERS HAVE TO DO WITH MANHOOD?

During the waning, lazy days of summer, I made some very biased and perhaps even sexist observations about how differently men and women relate to and judge themselves through food. Read on to find out what my mind does when it wonders and wanders …

On August 20, 2009, I took a few pepper samplers to school. They included habaneros, jalapeños, poblanos, and bells, and they were delivered to a few macho types at work. What is it about men, peppers, and hotness? Guys appear to measure their testosterone level by the heat level of the peppers they can consume. I am generalizing, I know, and I speak from observation, not from scientific research or out of any malice toward men. (I love men. After all, I am married to a man, I work with men, and I gave birth to three of them. So don't cry "sexist" just yet. Just wait a few more sentences … Then you may say it!) But it seems that what type car a man drives, what size hand or foot he has, and how many habaneros he can consume apparently equate to how manly he is. The sportier the car, the greater the correlation to a male's perceived wealth, status, physical stature, and power, or so it appears.

Might this compensate for a lack of maleness in other areas? I'm just saying! I observe and listen.

For us women, it appears that we measure our femininity by the number of products we can wear at one time: cologne, nail polish, false eyelashes, and rings. Our boob size, our weight, and our brand of clothing also serve as self-classifying mechanisms; that is, we judge ourselves based on the degree to which we fit the culturally accepted norms in all these areas. The style, quality, length, and texture of a woman's hair equate to unearned power in social realms. Dieting extremes like anorexia and bulimia are characteristic of wealth or higher social standing, while excess weight is equated with poverty; I think that the opposite was true a few hundred years ago. It now appears that the smaller dress size a woman wears, the wealthier, more privileged, or more beautiful society perceives her to be.

My bond with my garden found me sitting on my deck one sultry August day, looking out at the rows of vegetables and halfway listening to the television in the adjoining living room.

I watched red dragonflies seek food among the prickly leaves of my Japanese striped zucchini. One flew overhead, landing on the black wrought iron of my chair.

I listened to the senseless babble of vulture-like news reporters as they consumed the city of New Orleans in the aftermath of Hurricane Katrina, and I noticed my okra stalks, unnaturally full with screaming yellow blossoms, as they engulfed my pepper and tomato plants.

Chapter 6

FOOD AS LOVE ...

A *GOOD COOK,* host, or hostess makes the first move to welcome guests and strangers to partake of sustenance.

WHAT THE GOOD BOOK SAYS ...

In Luke 15:23 (King James Version), the father of the prodigal son says, "and bring hither the fatted calf and kill it; and let us eat and be merry." People of faith participate in the Lord's Supper or Holy Communion, physically partaking of food to symbolize God's reconciliation with us as saved sinners. Food is love, as Jesus's broken body is represented in the breaking of bread, and His blood, which freely flowed for our sins, is represented in the wine. The ultimate act of love is to know Him as our spiritual food and sustenance. Love is the food of the Living God—thus humanity's longing for feasting and infatuation with food. Bread and food permeate the fabric of all human cultures.

According to Isaiah 25:6, "And in this mountain shall the Lord of hosts make unto all people a feast of fat things, a feast of wines on the lees, of fat things full of marrow, of wines on the lees well refined." Food is not only necessary for life, it is life-giving; feasting and communal activities sustain people.

LIFE-GIVING FOODS

What did David eat? How about Paul? Or Jesus? Read the Bible to learn about our biblical culinary history and the context and use of these foods.

Biblical foods can be a basis for our present-day diet, too; the key is moderation and balance. Use the lines below to record your thoughts about the food references found in the Bible. I've filled in a few to get you started!

SEASONINGS, SPICES, AND HERBS

Anise (Matt. 23:23):   Tithes are paid with mint, anise, and cumin.

Coriander (Exod. 16:31; Num. 11:7):   Manna is described as tasting like coriander, and later like wafers made of honey.

Cinnamon (Exod. 30:23; Rev. 18:13):   God instructs Moses to take myrrh, cinnamon, and sweet calamus to the altar.

Cumin (Isa. 28:25; Matt. 23:23):   Cumin seeds are planted in the field.

Dill (Matt. 23:23):

Garlic (Num. 11:5):

Mint (Matt. 23:23; Luke 11:42):

Mustard (Matt. 13:31):

Rue (Luke 11:42):

Salt (Ezra 6:9; Job 6:6):

FRUIT AND NUTS

Apples (Song of Sol. 2:5):

Almonds (Gen. 43:11; Num. 17:8):

Dates (2 Sam. 6:19; 1 Chron. 16:3):

Figs (Neh. 13:15; Jer. 24:1–3): _____

Grapes (Lev. 19:10; Deut. 23:24): _____

Melons (Num. 11:5; Isa. 1:8): _____

Olives (Isa. 17:6; Mic. 6:15): _____

Pistachio nuts (Gen. 43:11): _____

Pomegranates (Num. 20:5; Deut. 8:8): _____

Raisins (Num. 6:3; 2 Sam. 6:19): _____

Sycamore fruit (Ps. 78:47; Amos 7:14): _____

Vegetables and Legumes

Beans (2 Sam. 17:28; Ezek. 4:9): _____

Cucumbers (Num. 11:5): _____

Gourds (2 Kings 4:39): _____

Leeks (Num. 11:5): _____

Lentils (Gen. 25:34; 2 Sam. 17:28; Ezek. 4:9): _____

Onions (Numbers 11:5) _____

GRAINS

Barley (Deut. 8:8; Ezek. 4:9): _____

Bread (Gen. 25:34; 2 Sam. 6:19, 16:1; Mark 8:14): _____

Corn (or grain, in King James Version) (Matt. 12:1): _____

Flour (2 Sam. 17:28; 1 Kings 17:12): _____

Millet (Ezek. 4:9): _____

Spelt (Ezek. 4:9): _____

Unleavened bread (Gen. 19:3; Exod. 12:20): _____

Wheat (Ezra 6:9; Deut. 8:8): _____

FISH

Matt. 15:36: _____

John 21:11–13: _____

FOWL

Partridge (1 Sam. 26:20; Jer. 17:11): _____

Pigeon (Gen. 15:9; Lev. 12:8): _____

Quail (Ps. 105:40): _____

Dove (Lev. 12:8): _____

MEAT

Calf (Prov. 15:17; Luke 15:23): _____

Goat (Gen. 27:9): _____

Lamb (2 Sam. 12:4): _____

Oxen (1 Kings 19:21): _____

Sheep (Deut. 14:4): _____

Venison (Gen. 27:7): _____

DAIRY

Butter (Prov. 30:33): _____

Cheese (2 Sam. 17:29; Job 10:10): _____

Curds (Isa. 7:15): _____

Milk (Exod. 33:3; Job 10:10; Judg. 5:25): _____

MISCELLANEOUS

Eggs (Job 6:6; Luke 11:12): _____

Grape juice (Num. 6:3): _____

Honey (Exod. 33:3; Deut. 8:8; Judg. 14:8–9): _____

Locust (Mark 1:6): _____

Olive oil (Ezra 6:9; Deut. 8:8): _____

Vinegar (Ruth 2:14; John 19:29): _____

Wine (Ezra 6:9; John 2:1–10): _____

Chapter 7

ME TO YOU: OUR FAVORITE MENUS

My sister Ruth and I are passionate about creating extravagant menus. We then set out on an adventure to make the best-tasting, most colorful meals we can. Here are a few menus from our past collaborations, starting with our backyard family feast from a July 4 gathering several years ago.

INDEPENDENCE DAY, 2005

Caramelized Onions, Mushrooms, and Chipped Beef on Buns

Bratwurst

Italian Sausage

Burgers

Baked Beans

Potato Salad

Tossed Salad

Chocolate Cake

Juneteenth (June 19) is a celebration that was founded in Galveston, Texas after the Civil War to commemorate the freeing of slaves. It is a big holiday for African-Americans in many southern states, and its traditions are passed from one generation to the next with a celebration of food and thanksgiving.

Ruth and I had so much fun making all the dishes for our Juneteenth celebration in 2005. We are especially proud of our tamarind fizzies, frozen drinks made with Jarritos, a Mexican brand of tamarind-flavored soda pop. We pour it into ice trays, freeze it, shave it into tall goblets, and add some cherry juice to top it off! We cook our ham hocks for several hours until they are falling off the bone, and then we add canned red beans, seasonings, and onions and cook them for another hour. Ron loves his peppers, so we add chopped jalapeños and drained canned corn to our corn bread before we bake it. We make sure to provide bowls of grated sharp cheddar and chopped green onions and bell peppers—sprinkled on top of a plate of beans and rice, they make for a delicious and memorable eating experience.

WHEN SISTAHS COOK – (JUNETEENTH 2005)

Fried Catfish Fillets

Fantail Fried Shrimp with Mustard and Plum Dipping Sauces

Red Beans with Ham Hocks and Rice, Topped with Grated Sharp Cheddar and Chopped Green Onions and Bell Peppers

Jalapeño Corn Bread Squares

Fruit Salad

Tamarind Fizzies

Beer-Battered Fried Zucchini

After Ruth and I visited Texas and Arizona, we decided it was time to merge our cuisine with that of the Southwest. The result is this festive menu:

A Tribute to the Southwest

Black Bean, Corn, Pepper, and Onion Salsa

Chicken Cheese Wraps

Sausage Chalupas

Mango Salad

Lemonade Coolers

Dr. King's strength of character prompted me to celebrate this great man by making a special MLK Day meal for my husband. The dishes celebrate diversity. My grilled fruit is simple but satisfying: I season freshly sliced fruit with cardamom and then place it on the grill for just a few moments to bring forth its sugars.

Martin Luther King, Jr. Day – At Home with a T-Bone Dinner

T-Bone Steaks, Oven-Broiled with Steak Sauce and Onions

Saffron Rice with Toasted Almonds, Dried Cranberries, and Artichoke Hearts

Grilled Zucchini, Yellow Squash, Carrots, and Onions

Stewed or Grilled Fruit: Pears, Apples, Mangoes, and Oranges, Seasoned with Cardamom and Served with Light Brown Sugar Topping

Three-Cheese Biscuits

No menu is complete without a list of our family's favorite sweets. Among them is Momma's mile-high banana pudding with vanilla wafers and sweet milk custard, and her bread pudding, which has been modified with day-old doughnuts, French bread cubes, dried cherries, and rum, and topped off with caramel sauce. (More favorites just might appear in a future cookbook!)

OUR FAVORITE DESSERTS

Banana Pudding with Meringue

Bread Pudding with Caramel Sauce

Coconut Cake with Lemon Filling

Blackberry Cobbler

Peach Cobbler

Plain Butter Cake

Cheesecake (Diane's recipe)

Double Chocolate and White Chocolate Chip Cookies

7-Up Cake

Oatmeal Raisin Cookies

Piña Colada Zucchini Bread

Rum Oatmeal Chocolate Walnut Cookies

Peanut Butter Cookies

Rum Cardamom Sugar Cookies

Diane on Tybee Island, Georgia, 2010: Great Low Country food, hospitality, and the beautiful Atlantic—life doesn't get any better than this! (Personal photo)

My siblings and I grew up in Jacksonville, Florida, and we often went fishing with our mom and dad at Mayport Beach, St. Augustine, and Little Talbot Island—excursions from living in "the circle." They were lean times, and we lacked many things. What we didn't lack was the understanding that our condition wasn't permanent. We were told that we could do all things. I believed that then, and I still believe it today.

Since then, I've learned to look back on those times with a sense of humor and a renewed appreciation for my humble beginnings. Food, poverty, and a "make do" approach to living out hard times gave birth to some really unique events and creations!

- We were so poor that when we ran out of hair grease, my brother used Crisco to oil his hair!
- We were so poor that we'd do "plate trades" with our friends, who were poor, too! These trades were made blindly with the hope that someone had a better dinner than you. With a *good* trade, you might get fried chicken, sausages, macaroni and cheese, green beans, candied yams, fish, cornbread … you know, the good stuff. Or you might get a *bad* trade: pig snouts with mustard, hog mawgs, chittlins, sweetbreads, or pig tails! (Once my sister's friend wanted to trade her dinner—a fried pig tail sandwich.)
- We were so poor that our brother's soon-to-be-girlfriend, who was also poor, came to his old car eating the ultimate "hood food"—a neck bone sandwich! My sister and I were in the backseat, cracking up with laughter, and my sister said, "How in the hell can she eat that?" She was making reference to the bones sticking out of the light bread.
- We were so poor that when we ran out of jelly, we made sugar sandwiches.

Chapter 8

DADDY

DADDY USED TO hunt for rodents and other "wild" food. Momma never wanted him to cook these untamed dishes, but to him there was something about capturing and cooking these wild creatures that satisfied his inner hunter. My siblings and I still remember so many of Daddy's cooking adventures.

ROADKILL RECIPE

1 rodent/scavenger (possum, raccoon, turtle, snake, gator, or rabbit), skinned, OR parts of said rodent/scavenger

1 cup insanity

2 cups living in the backwoods of Georgia—or too close to the swamp

½ T courage

2 rounds buckshot

Season to taste. Hand-mix, using a seventy-seven-year-old granddaddy. Make sure he has a pickled pig foot and a bottle of beer, and watch both simmer. (Do not disturb until both dish and cook are highly elevated!) Sample and add salt and pepper to taste. Enjoy the fricassee, and smile while eating … just like Daddy.

Daddy died in the Spring of 1999. I miss him, and I treasure his last words, about the 'coon he had in a cage in the backyard: "I got a coon … he's out there getting fat … he's pretty, too." Daddy was very knowledgeable about his food, but I never wanted to be that personal with mine, naming it or having it for a pet—ugh!

Daddy never finished school beyond the third grade. He lost his mother to tuberculosis around age six. His life as the son of a sharecropper during the 1920s and '30s in rural Vidalia, Georgia, was hard and unforgiving. His daddy, Granddaddy Elisha Wells, was long on conversation and telling great tales.. He was hell-bent on achieving something, but the fact is, life was hardscrabble for Granddaddy, a widowed sharecropper with four children. It was difficult for a single man in 1931 to raise four children and make a living, too. Consequently, Granddaddy brought home a mean old woman to help care for my daddy and his brothers and sister. Daddy told my siblings and me about the mean things she did to them and how he would run away into the woods, where he found peace as a hunter of 'coons, rabbits, and possums. Wild things brought a certain amount of calm to Daddy. I think he grieved for his momma most of his life, but he was unable to express that pain to others.

He was, however, a great storyteller. Daddy told us stories about hunting, making moonshine in a still, and tapping pine trees for sap. He also told us some out-an-out rural legends … I think to scare the baheebie-jeebies out of us! Like the one about the traveling foreigner he invited in for dinner when my second-oldest brother was a baby. Momma and Daddy were farmers at the time, and as all farmers do, they had cats to keep away the mice. Well, this foreigner, according to my daddy, spotted one of the cats and made the comment, "Whooo-*whee*! That kitty show would be good with some rice!" Momma heard his comment, turned to Daddy, and said, "Clarence, get that man out of our house. The next thing you know, he might want to eat the baby!" Needless to say, Daddy showed him the door. Laughter was usually involved in Daddy's "believe-it-or-not" style of telling tales out of school.

Daddy also was the first rapper that I knew of. When intoxicated on seal whiskey, he would talk a whole lot of trash! (Side note: Daddy distinguished store-bought whiskey as "seal whiskey" and mason jar moonshine as a "drink of shine." Remember, Daddy grew up during Prohibition and knew of backwoods "shine" way before he ever went to a bar.) Anyway, once he'd loaded up with shine on a Friday evening, after eating some fried mullet fish or some greasy ribs, Daddy would rap: "Tall like a pine, black like a crow, I can talk more trash than any radio!" Daddy had a unique laugh—a *cuh, cuh, cuh* sound blended with full-bodied jovialness. I can see him now, laughing, wearing his bib overalls, cotton shirt, brown wingtip shoes, and wide-brimmed hat.

Once when he made a giant pot of collard greens, he argued with Momma because he didn't want to waste the stems, and he added them to the pot. It looked more like a pot of green water with floating giant green worms. Ruth and I cried because we didn't want to eat it.

And then there was the time he brought home some chicken feet to cook. I had gone away to college, and Ruth told me that Daddy had planned on cooking them for the family to eat. My mother was furious. But Daddy did cook those chicken feet. Thank goodness I wasn't there to eat them with my siblings! James Brown used to sing a song about "Poppa don't take no mess …" Well, our poppa sure could cook up a mess of chicken feet!

Okay, let's test our rapping skills using Daddy's words. Try your hand at making this into a rap:

DADDY'S RAP

Daddy don't eat no cats.

He's just too cool for that.

Daddy only drinks shine in a jar.

He never goes to the store in a car.

His rap is cool

though he didn't finish school!

Before "No Reservations," Daddy didn't have any.

We didn't have a lot, but stories we had aplenty!

'Cause Daddy could tell a tale

every Friday night without fail!

He was the original OG

way before we had color TV.

He entertained us with his rural tales

of creepy visitors and people in jail.

Each time he spoke

we'd laugh so hard we'd almost choke

on a chicken foot!

—to Daddy, from Diane

Chapter 9

A TRIBUTE TO MOMMA

MOMMA, *ELIZABETH FULLER* Wells, was an amazing human being. She was witty and could crack jokes with old and young alike. Her famous 7-Up Cake was known and relished by all my brothers and sisters and their friends, too. Often my brother Melvin would buy Momma butter and cake flour so he could have his own personal cake instead of the usual hunk of a slice taken from Momma's cake plate. During her later years, she was known for making a cake a day. My sons Chris and Marc would get off the school bus anticipating her double-decker, chocolate-laden, high-calorie delights.

Momma never waited for her cakes to cool before frosting them. She would slather the frosting on the Bundt-shaped cakes while they were still hot from the oven, and it would drip down the sides and center. Once, I gently suggested she wait to frost her cake until it cooled down, and she quickly reminded me that the grandkids loved it that way—especially the "extra" frosting on the side when she served it up!

Ruth and I have used the same ingredients Momma did to make beautifully frosted creations, only to hear our children complain that our cakes were not like Grandma Lizzy's. There is a southern saying, "She put her foot in it up to her knees"—meaning someone put her best efforts to the task at hand. That describes how Momma approached cooking, and our children sensed that, drawing love and comfort from her culinary efforts each day. Momma took the time to make dessert a prerequisite for each meal.

Strangers and neighbors alike took to Momma's cooking. From her smothered chicken and rice and her turkey pie to her pork chops and onions and her collard greens, food was always a focus when we visited Momma. She made a way out of "no way" for us when we were growing up, and as we became adults, we gave back in return—buying her nice things, taking her fishing, and purchasing food for her to cook for us. Even as adults we just knew Momma could add something to shrimp fried rice or turkey pie that no restaurant or TV dinner could do!

My husband, Ron, particularly enjoyed the homemade turkey pies Momma would make for him after Thanksgiving. The two of them had a bond that stretched beyond that of son- and mother-in-law. They complimented one another, congratulating each another on their weight loss, and generally showed mutual kindness that transcended in-law stereotypes and gave Momma a bit of brightness. Momma's diabetes took its final toll on her in 2000.

One of Momma's idiosyncrasies was her odd food pairings, which seemed to be made for her taste buds only. Momma taught me through example to eat the following (save one item that I will never, never, ever, *ever* eat):

- sardines and soda crackers with hot sauce
- purlough rice and turkey necks
- neck bones and black-eyed peas
- mullet fish and grits
- mayonnaise and grape jelly sandwiches (Momma called these her "sweet and sour sandwiches"—ugh!)

One of Momma's habits—infamous among us kids—was piling all our food onto one plate. This included dessert. Thus, potato salad, collard green juice, rice, gravy, chicken, and chocolate cake all merged on our plates. I suspect she did this to save on the number of dishes she had to use for all eleven of us! I think that over the years, Daddy learned to avoid the merger by having each item on a separate plate … I used to wonder why he got three or four plates on the dinner table, while we all had just one. (Side note: Daddy also ate peas with a butter knife. I think that this was a culinary skill, or perhaps just an odd habit, to demonstrate his balancing prowess and satisfy his need for showmanship.) My youngest sister took after Daddy and favors compartmentalized plates when she eats. I simply avoid the merger and serve dessert last. Neither one of us has taken up eating peas with a butter knife!

Momma spent her last Sunday with Ron and me, eating Sunday dinner and then lying down to take a nap. I covered her with a quilt that I had made, and then I called my sister. Momma went back home with Ruth and died in her sleep later that Sunday night. We are so grateful to have had Momma for seventy-five years. What she taught us in words, deeds, and examples is more precious than college degrees and social status. Momma, we all miss you and love you!

Chapter 10

RECIPES FROM OUR FAVORITE MENUS

MY FAVORITE MEAL is a bowl of rice and beans, a thick slice of zucchini bread, and a nice, tall glass of slushy tamarind fizzie. These recipes can be modified to suit individual tastes. I usually serve some type of bean soup when I have co-workers or friends over to my home. We love the warmth and hearty flavors found in the soups, as well as the juicy morsels of ham.

Enjoy making these recipes with your family, and invite a few friends to join you. I am sure they will rush right over—and ask for seconds.

Piña Colada Zucchini Bread

3 eggs

½ cup vegetable oil

½ stick butter

2 cups white sugar

2 cups grated zucchini

1 small can crushed pineapple (do not drain)

2 cups grated moist coconut

2 t vanilla extract

3 cups all-purpose flour

3 t ground cinnamon

1 t baking soda

¼ t baking powder

1 t salt

½ cup chopped walnuts

1. Preheat oven to 325°F. Grease and flour two 8 x 4 in. loaf pans.
2. In a large bowl, beat eggs until light and frothy. Mix in oil, sugar, and pineapple. Stir in zucchini and vanilla. Combine flour, cinnamon, baking soda, baking powder, salt, nuts, and coconut; stir into the egg mixture. Divide batter into prepared pans.
3. Bake 60–70 minutes, or until done. Cool and wrap in clear plastic. Slice and serve with cream cheese or jam.

RED BEANS WITH HAM HOCKS AND RICE

3 cans red beans (15 oz. each)

1–3 lbs. smoked ham hocks

3 cups basmati rice, cooked

1 cup cooked mashed potatoes

2 cups grated sharp cheddar cheese

1 cup chopped green onion

2 cups chopped yellow onions

2 cups chopped green bell pepper

1t red pepper flakes

2 whole garlic cloves, crushed

½ t oregano

1 T ground black pepper

½ t crushed sage

salt to taste

In a large stew pot, cook smoked ham hocks in 3 cups of water, along with the yellow onions, 1 cup chopped bell pepper, garlic, and other seasonings. Bring to a boil, reduce heat, and simmer for 2 hours. Remove the skin and bones from the ham hocks, chop the ham, and return it to the pot. Add the beans, cook 20 more minutes, and then add the mashed potatoes. Cook another 10 minutes. Serve the cooked basmati rice in bowls, and top with generous portions of the beans and ham hocks. Garnish with grated sharp cheddar, chopped green onions, and chopped bell pepper. Serves 9–10.

TAMARIND FIZZIES

1 bottle (12.5 oz.) Jarritos tamarind-flavored drink

1 cup ginger ale

2 T maraschino cherry liquid

Mix all ingredients in a plastic pitcher and freeze in a bowl or ice tray. Shave or thaw slightly and serve in champagne glasses with a cherry on top. Serves 1–2.

About the Author

DIANE WELLS RIVERS holds a Doctor of Education degree in Pre-K-12 Administration and Supervision. She has traveled to Japan and West Germany. She is passionate about designing wearable yarn items, quilting, acrylic painting and food. She has been an outstanding educator for twenty-nine years. Her favorite artists are Faith Ringgold, Georgia O'Keeffe, Nicholas Rivers, and Gabriel Rivers. Dr. Rivers is currently working on a collection of tales about school and a non-fiction book for urban teachers.

Printed in the United States
by Baker & Taylor Publisher Services